Ancient Writing on Metal Plates

Ancient Writing on Metal Plates

Archaeological Findings Support Mormon Claims

Paul R. Cheesman

International Standard Book Number
0-88290-303-9

Library of Congress Catalog Card Number
85-080179

Horizon Publishers Catalog and Order Number
1002

Printed and Distributed in the
United States of America
by

Horizon
Publishers
& Distributors, Incorporated

50 South 500 West
P.O. Box 490
Bountiful, Utah 84010

Dedicated to
Elder Mark E. Petersen
whose friendship and encouragement
in this research project
increased my understanding of its importance.

Contents

Preface

The Book of Mormon is a magnificent ancient record which links Christianity of the Old World with Christianity in the New World. It is the extended story of some of the house of Israel in the New World.

The Book of Mormon is an abridged record of three groups of people who migrated from the Old World. The first group, known as the Jaredites, came in approximately 2400 B.C., while the other two groups arrived about 600 B.C. The book contains a religious history of God's dealings with them. Those to whom God spoke were commanded to write the information (1 Nephi 14:25). Some of the messages given by the leaders were copied and circulated. All of this activity therefore infers (1) that a language was spoken, (2) that some form of writing was used, and (3) at least some of the people were civilized, educated, and informed.

With this background and claim, the Book of Mormon is unique, since (until recently) the general opinion of scholars was that the Indians and their ancestors had no writing system or any means of recording information. In this regard, therefore, a discussion on the possibility of ancient writing in the New World merits our attention.

The claim of The Church of Jesus Christ of Latter-day Saints is that Joseph Smith translated a record found on gold plates, written laboriously by some of the ancestors of the American Indian. Therefore, these people had a knowledge of writing with this particular record written on metal plates.

At the time of Joseph Smith's remarkable discovery in 1830, there was probably no knowledge of writing amongst the American Indians, or of any written on metal. In fact, it is evident that a knowledge of any ancient culture writing on metal, anywhere in the world, was not public knowledge at that time.

Since 1830, however, numerous examples of ancient writing have been found in the Old World. If the ancestors of the

American Indian, or at least some of them as suggested by the Book of Mormon, came from the Old World, we can assume that they would bring the customs and traditions of their home-land with them. In America, Joseph Smith stood alone in his bold declaration that he had found:

1. an ancient record written in an Egyptian language which had been re-formed and condensed.
2. a record engraved on thin sheets of gold.
3. a record bound with metal rings.
4. a record placed in a stone box.

Similarities of Writing in the Old World and the New World

Ancient Language in the New World

In the Old World as well as the New, the origin of writing is often ascribed to divinity (J. Gelb, *A Study of Writing*, p. 231). Therefore, its development should encompass all mankind.

The great variety of Indian languages—although it is known that they diverged through the millennia from a smaller number of parent tongues of very ancient times—also bespeak many peoples. To date, it has not been possible to determine how many different languages and dialects have been spoken in the Americas, as many tongues have become extinct. But Morris Swades, a linguistic scholar, estimates that when the Anglos arrived in the New World, Indians were speaking some 2,200 different languages, or dialects, with many regional variations. Other scholars have estimated that there were at least 200 mutually unintelligible languages among the native people north of Mexico, with at least another 350 in Mexico and Central America, and considerably more than 1,000 in the Caribbean and South America (Alvin M. Josephy, Jr., *The Indian Heritage of America*, p. 12).

Statements in the Book of Mormon reveal the language of that record. Nephi, the founder of the Nephite nation, wrote: "I made a record in the language of my father (Lehi) which consists of the learning of the Jews [verbal concepts] and the language [characters of verbal symbols] of the Egyptians" (Nephi 1:2). In commenting on the education of the sons of one of the kings (Mosiah) some 400 years later, Mormon, the editor, writes:

For it were not possible that our father, Lehi, could have re-membered all these things to have taught them to his children, except it were for the help of these plates; for he having been taught in the language of the Egyptians, therefore he could read these engravings and teach them to his children that thereby they could teach them to their children. (Mosiah 1:4)

His son, Moroni, the final editor of the Book of Mormon (fifth century A.D.), records:

And now, behold, we have written this record according to our knowledge in the characters which are called among us Reformed Egyptian being handed down and altered by us ac-cording to our manner of speech; and if our plates had been suf-ficiently large we should have written in Hebrew, but the Hebrew hath been altered by us also; and if we could have written in Hebrew, behold we would have had no imperfection in our record. (Mormon 9:32-33)

Helaman adds:

And now there are many records kept of the proceedings of this people, by many of this people, which are particular and very large, concerning them. But behold, a hundredth part of the proceeding of this people, yea, the account of the Lamanites and of the Nephites . . . cannot be contained in this work. But behold, there are many books and many records of every kind, and they have been kept chiefly by the Nephites. (Helaman 3:13-15)

The Book of Mormon indicates that a language was taught by the people:

And he appointed teachers of the brethren of Amulon in every land which was possessed by his people; and thus the language of Nephi began to be taught among all the people of the Lamanites. (Mosiah 24:4)

And it came to pass that he [Benjamin] began to speak to his people from the tower; and they could not hear his words because of the greatness of the multitude; therefore he caused that the words which he spake should be *written* and sent forth among those that were not under the sound of his voice, that they might also receive his words. (Mosiah 2:8; italics added)

The Book of Mormon makes over a hundred references to "writing" (George Reynolds, *A Complete Concordance of the Book of Mormon*, p. 823).

It is possible that the circulated message was written on some type of lightweight, portable material.

> Those engravings which were in the possession of Helaman were written and sent forth among the children of men throughout all the land. (Alma 63:12; 51:15)

The Hopi language has one word for airplane; we have many. The Aztec has one word for cold or cold wind, snow, or ice. The Eskimo has twenty-two terms just for snow. The English language has many words for movement; the Hopi is interested in only slow or fast motion. The Spanish language has feminine or masculine gender; the English does not (except we do call a ship a she). In English, you can understand an idea only by a further idea.

Some have described the Maya language as musical and pleasant. Letters from our speech such as "d," "f," and "r" are absent. The Mayas wrote simple sentences and were weak in verbs.

Cyrus Gordon believes that the comparison which Pierre Honore makes between the Mayan and Cretan are too detailed to be brushed aside (Cyrus H. Gordon, *Before Columbus*, p. 92).

Today the most widely used Indian tongue is Quechua, spoken by approximately eight million Indians in Peru, Ecuador, Bolivia, South Colombia, and northern Argentina. Mayan is the second in preference and spoken by about two million people in Guatemala and Mexico. Other tribal languages still spoken are Aymara (Bolivia, Peru, northern Chile); Gurani (Paraguay, small areas of Bolivia, and Brazil); Nahuatl (Mexico and San Salvador) and Optopame (Mexico) (CNRS Research 6, 1977, p. 17).

Gloria Farley, president of the Eastern Oklahoma Historical Society, has for years carefully recorded evidences from Mississippi tributaries of the southeast of pre-Columbian contacts.

Singlehandedly, she has catalogued over fifty inscriptions in nine unique languages, including several drawings of ships.

Dr. Barry Fell, president of the Epigraphic Society, finds a direct relationship between writing in America to Celtic, Iberic, Punic, Hebrew, and Egyptian. He believes the earliest writing in America is approximately 1450 B.C.

Bernard Pottier, professor of the Institute of Hispanic Studies in Paris, wrote, "Was writing known in the Americas? The answer is yes" (*The Indian Languages of America* in Research, pp. 15-19).

A technique known as "blottochronology," or Lexicostatistics, has been developed by American linguists in studying North American Indian languages. It was found that the words from certain key basic objects and concepts in American Indian languages tended to be impervious to borrowings from unrelated languages. An example is of words like sun, knife, woman, and low numerals. The rate of change of such core words were relatively constant, at about twenty percent per 1,000 years.

On May 17, 1960, a UPI report released by the Columbian Anthropology Commission, printed in the Cuban newspaper, *Information*, told of Hebrew and Chinese letter-characters which had been found in the LaMacarena mountain range. Ten years later the *Miami Herald* reported the finding of Mayan-like hieroglyphics in a cave on the Dutch Antilles island of Bonaire.

The word "quilcas," which was used by the Incas, refers to writing. It meant "one who knows how to read and write with instruments of reading and writing." Paper and letters are referred to in this definition (Gilda Corgorno Venture, *Revista de la Biblio teca Nacional Instituto Nacional de Culture*, Lima, Peru, Nos. 24/25, 1974/1975, published 1977).

Studies on ancient writing indicate that there are four hundred different writing systems known, and nineteen of them are used in our day. Those who are currently studying Peruvian writing conclude that logographic systems, as well as the alphabet, are different stages of the development of graphic writing. The basic principle of the Peruvian writing was a square or rectangle which was modified internally by the addition of lines, points, circles, and changes of color. The Hittite system in Turkey is somewhat similar. This point is emphasized because an *alphabet system* is abstract, whereas in *graphic systems* the drawings can reveal a relationship.

In South America the dominant language at the time of the Spanish Conquest was Chimu. This language evolved from the Mochica Culture in Peru and was modified by them.

The formal domain of writing is in the hand of the paleographer and epigrapher. By definition, the paleographer studies mainly manuscripts on skin, papyrus, or paper written in, drawn, or painted characters. The epigrapher is interested chiefly in inscriptions incised with a sharp tool on hard material such as stone, wood, metal, or clay.

The highly developed calendar system of ancient America emerges as a unique achievement among the other cultural accomplishments of the pre-Columbians. These systems were incised on stone and metal.

It seems that the formal aspect of writing would appear to have progressed to a considerably higher degree among the Aztecs and Mayas than among the North American Indian.

Many scholars are of the opinion that "Naturally there was a time when man did not know how to write" (I. J. Gelb, *A Study of Writing*, p. 24). The Mormons take a different view, however, and substantiate this conviction with the statements in the Book of Mormon which they consider canonized scripture.

At the time of the Spanish conquerors, the Mayas had in their possession a national library of literature, science, and history in the form of books using their hieroglyphic characters. Some of these may have explained their origin, and named the exact place where their first date stone was erected, also the location of the original development of their marvelous civilization, and why it was brought to Yucatan and developed such a high degree of civilization. Their particular culture survived for fifteen hundred years before it was destroyed by the conquerors; but due to the energy of the first missionaries and their zeal to supplant the Maya religion with a Christian faith, their great and treasured library vanished into flames.

Besides the Mesoamerican texts referring to astronomical events and celestial deities, new research now reveals that these records included information concerning dynasties, genealogies, wars, and tributes. Other ancestors of the American Indian have indicated that priests or scribes kept records of ages past (Constance Irwin, *Fair Gods and Stone Faces*, p. 34).

Research now indicates that during a certain period in the history of Peru, the people were forbidden to write. An ancient chronicle reads as follows:

> . . . Tupac Canri commanded by law that under the pain of death no one should traffic in quilcas, which were the parchment and leaves of trees on which they used to write, nor should use any sort of letters. They observed this oracular command with so much care that after this loss the Peruvians never used letters. And because in later times a learned amanta invented some characters, they burnt him alive, and so, from this time forth, they used threads and quipa (kee-pu). (Fernando Montestnos, *Memorias Antiquas Historiales del Peru*, p. 64)

Languages of the Old World Found in the New World

If the Book of Mormon is an English translation of a record written by a people originating from a Hebrew-speaking community, it seems there should be found within its pages the grammatical structure, as well as the expressions and thinking processes of the Hebrew language as translated into the English tongue. A Hebrew idiom is defined in its broadest sense as any peculiar character of the area of Jerusalem. Since Hebrew was the language of that area then, it may be supposed that Lehi spoke Hebrew. There are indications that 1,000 years after Lehi's time, his American descendants were still acquainted with that language (Mormon 9:33).

A cursory count of the vocabulary in the Book of Mormon reveals approximately 2,696 word roots—adjectives are rarely used. This is one of the characteristics of the Hebrew language.

Hebrew syntax is relatively simple because of the ever-recurring "and." Only a few verses of the Small Plates are needed to convince the reader that this pattern of Hebrew syntax is followed. "And" often stands before each word or phrase in a series in the Book of Mormon, possibly because there was no punctuation. Genesis 20:14 and 1 Samuel 13:20 illustrate the same usage in the Bible. The style of enumeration in the Book of Mormon follows the principles of othe Hebrew language extensively. Numbers composed of tens and units, e.g., 23, usually appear in the older writings with the larger number first and the two numbers joined by "and," therefore, twenty-and-three (A. B. Davidson, *Hebrew Syntax*, p. 54).

In the use of prepositions and prepositional phrases used in the Small Plates, these expressions meet the requirements of correct Hebrew usage. "Before the wind" (1 Nephi 11:1), "into an exceeding high mountain" (1 Nephi 11:1) are not uncommon usages in the Old Testament (Exodus 24:12, 13; Numbers 27:12; Deuteronomy 10:1).

In the Small Plates, a man takes a woman to be his wife and records it in characteristic Hebrew; e.g., "his sons should take daughters to wife" (1 Nephi 7:1). In Hebrew a man does not marry a woman but he "takes her to wife" or "she is given to him to wife" (John McFadyen, *Key to Introductory Hebrew Grammar*, p. 13).

"By the hand of" is found in the singular form many times in the Small Plates (1 Nephi 5:14; 13:26; 2 Nephi 1:5, 6; Jacob 1:18). This is a very interesting Hebrew phrase which shows instrumentality, and is common in the Old Testament (Exodus 9:35, 1 Samuel 28:15).

The construct form of adjectival phrase, e.g., "an iron rod," is handled differently from the English manner. In Hebrew, consequently, the correct form would be "rod of iron." The translation of the Small Plates has been rather consistent in this respect. "Rod of iron" is used eight times in this fashion and never as the "iron rod"; "house of Laban" and "the daughters of Ishmael" are other examples of this form.

It can be said that the construct form in Hebrew is a very common grammatical structure, and

> . . . if we find . . . that there is more than the customary resort as English practice goes, to the equivalent form with an apostrophe to denote the possessor, that fact will put the Book of Mormon on a basis which is distinctly Jewish in this particular aspect, and tends strongly to show that no English author wrote that book. (Thomas W. Brockbank, *Improvement Era*, XVII, 1914, p. 1061)

One observes in the Small Plates an unusual practice of making many nouns plural which would seem to require the singular form. This practice is not alien to proper Hebrew usage as indicated by examining the Old Testament (E. Craig Bramwell, *Hebrew Idioms in the Small Plates of Nephi* [thesis], Brigham Young University, 1960).

One interesting example of plural nouns found in the Book of Mormon is 1 Nephi 16:21. Nephi writes that the steel bows had "lost their springs." This is the Semitic use of a plural for a noun of quality.

The grammatical principle of the compound subject is illustrated in the Old Testament and the Small Plates; e.g., "I and my brethren" (1 Kings 1:21; 1 Samuel 14:40; Genesis 43:8; 1 Nephi 3:9, 10; 5:30; 7:2, 3:22; 22:31). This is immediately recognized as being poor English grammatical construction, but it can be defended by its Hebrew origin.

The expression, "and it came to pass," is as frequently employed in the Hebrew text of the Old Testament as in the Book of Mormon. This phrase could be equal to our period— the end of one thought and the beginning of another.

This short summary of the Hebrew idioms in the Small Plates can be supplemented in the study made by E. Craig Bramwell in his Brigham Young University thesis Idioms in the Small Plates of Nephi," 1960.

In support of the theory that the Indians are descendants of the Hebrew nation, Elijah M. Haines summarizes the opinion of many archaeologists:

The languages of the Indians and of the Hebrews . . . are both found without prepositions, and are formed with prefixes and suffixes, a thing not common to other languages; and he says that not only words but the construction of phrases in both are essentially the same. The Indian pronoun, as well as other nouns, . . . are manifestly from the Hebrews. The Indian laconic, bold, and commanding figures of speech, . . . exactly agreeing with the genius of the Hebrew language. (Elijah M. Hanes, *The American Indian*, p. 99)

Concerning Haines' comments as cited above, the writer is cognizant that most students of this discipline acknowledge that there is no such language as "Indian." There are many Indian languages divided among the various tribes.

Forms of Writing

The science of writing is now being given the name of grammatology. With such sophistication, forms of communication are broken down into visual, audible, and written. Some written symbols, such as pictures, become pictographs and are not considered by some as "writing." Others specify that to qualify for the classification of writing, the system must have an alphabet. A rebus is any style of writing in which the letters are so arranged as to suggest a picture of the topic to which the writing relates. This is shown in advertising, for example, when a baker will place a sign above his shop in which the word "bread" is formed in the shape of a loaf of bread.

Most civilizations used an idea form of writing; that is, they used a symbol to express an idea or thought rather than an alphabet. Chinese and Egyptian are prime examples of this type of writing. The Maya glyphs are also an example of an idea form of writing in the New World.

Most ancient civilization seems to have preferred a thought symbol to an alphabetical system. It may have been that only the priestly class and civic officials utilized the system of writing we found in ancient America.

One of the most important writing systems in the Americas is from the Cherokee Indian tribe. It was invented by an Indian named Sequoyah for use among his tribesmen living in North Carolina. Sequoyah could not read or write English but saw the necessity of having a language. He, therefore, organized a system of semasiography-pictographic signs each of which stood for words of his tongue. These he developed into syllables, and substituted forms of letters instead of pictures. Thus, he created a syllabary of some two hundred signs, later simplifying it to eighty-five.

The Maya inscriptions are still being catalogued as they are found. It is estimated that Mayan hieroglyphic writing was based on 400 to 600 individual glyphs which sometimes stood alone but more often appeared as two or more. The numerical system was comparatively easy to discern, the calendar systems complicated, but have been unraveled. Other glyphs, too mysterious to discern, are still a puzzlement to yet a new generation of interpreters. Some scholars are now attempting to interpret an inscription from Palenque, Mexico, with 600 glyphs which begin in one structure and continue in two other buildings. These new translators believe that in time they can put the story together. This particular inscription is dated A.D. 321 (*Scientific American*, May 1978, pp. 95, 96).

Father Diego de Landa described the books of Yucatan soon after the Spanish conquest:

> These people also made use of certain characters or letters with which they wrote in their books their ancient matters and their sciences, and by these drawings and by certain signs in these drawings, they understood their affairs and made others understand them and taught them. (*Relacion de last Cosa de Yucatan*, translation A. M. Tozer, ed., pp. 27,28)

Of this extensive corpus of Maya texts, fifty percent remains undeciphered. Those glyphs which deal with dates and calculations can be read; but those which describe ritual and history are currently in the process of being interpreted.

The written or inscribed language of the Aztecs was very different from that of the Mayas. Whereas the Mayas used symbols and various characters which in no way related to the subject, the Aztecs, however, employed pictographs of the subject accompanied by numerical or other symbols. The Mayas mainly employed glyphs cut into stone for recording events (with their codices or pictoglyphs being of secondary importance), while the Aztecs used codices almost exclusively.

In addition to these methods of communication, when recording calendrical matters they used various signs or symbols of the days, names of deities, etc., with such records often carved on stone. Although these are far easier to decipher than those of the Mayas, yet there are many matters on which archaeologists do not agree. We cannot state positively why various representations of some one deity should be very different in details. Neither can we be certain that the correct meanings have been given many of the signs and symbols.

In some instances the Phoenicians and the Mayans used similar characters for the same letters and also similar meanings for the characters. Pierre Honore's studies conclude that the Phoenician and Mayan scripts have a common root older than the Phoenician script from which they both developed (Pierre Honore, In Quest of the White God, p. 37).

In a letter from C. S. Rafinesque to Champollion in 1832, he identifies ten varieties of script or writing systems which are present in the Americas among the aboriginal population:

1. Symbols or glyphs of the Toltecs, Aztecs, Huastecs, Skeres, Panos, etc. These are supposed to resemble early Chinese characters.
2. Outlines of figures or abridged symbols and glyphs (petroglyphs)
3. Quipus and other knotted string systems
4. Wampum, shell, or bead strings and belts
5. Runic glyphs or marks and notches on twigs or lines used by several nations of North America—similar to the runic glyphs of Celtic or Teutonic nations
6. Runic marks and dots, or graphic symbols, not on strings or lines, but in rows, used by Talegas, Aztecs, Natchez,

Powhatan, Tuscarora, Muiscas of Colombia—similar to Egyptian, Etruscan, Celtic symbols
7. Maya glyphs on stelae—similar to ancient Libyan, Egyptian, Persian, and Chinese
8. Maya glyphs on codices
9. Syllabic letters, Cherokee alphabet, other systems from North and South America
10. Modern alphabets on medals, coins found throughout the Americas in ancient contexts.

(Josiah Priest, *American Antiquities*, 3rd ed. revised.)

Pictoglyphs and petroglyphs are pictorial symbols which record certain events and provide another method of communication. Examples of this form of writing have been found throughout the southwestern United States. Many interpretations of the symbols are available. However, no key exists which provides exact definitions for all these colorful character-glyph writings.

F. A. Mason observed that during the period of 300 B.C. to 500 B.C. the ancient Peruvians had some form of writing. He believed this to be nonverbal, and not alphabetic, phonetic, syllabic, or probably even pictographic. He concluded that the message, however, was apparently incised on lima beans and could be interpreted only by a special class of people trained in such decipherment. Mason admitted that he did not know how standard these ideograms were (J. Alden Mason, *The Ancient Civilizations of Peru*, p. 73).

Dr. Wells Jakeman points to the numerous ancient hieroglyphs discovered in the Maya area of Mexico which do not yet provide a key to the written history of that group. Quoting from another source, Dr. Jakeman observes as follows:

The Maya hieroglyphs were evidently pictorial in origin, but had become so conventionalized and stylized that in few cases is the meaning apparent. . . . The meanings of only a small proportion of these glyphs are known, but those that can be interpreted recur most frequently. Those identifiable glyphs all refer to calendrical, astronomical, and arithmetical data, and thus only the calendrical content of most inscriptions can be understood. . . . In some portions there may be an approximation to true writing; this is especially true of the native written books or codices, only three of which have survived (Wells Jakeman, *The Ancient Civilizations of Middle America*, pp. 37, 38, 207).

In 1966, author Clark Wissler wrote:

The Maya and Aztec did have some written literature. (*Indians of the United States*, p. 147)

And in connection with this literature, it is also Wissler's opinion that there is some evidence that the Inca cultivated the drama—that the early peoples of Mexico achieved some status in dramatic arts (*Ibid.*, p. 145).

Other authorities characterize the Mayan civilization as having developed a genuine written language, or something approximating hieroglyphic ideographs. These conventionalized symbols represented certain words, as does Chinese writing, or quite possibly they (some scholars disagree) represented phonetic syllables or sounds, as in the case of our own alphabet (Editors of *The American Heritage of America*, p. 19).

An early Spanish priest, Bishop Diego de Landa, recorded some interesting information regarding the records of the pre-Spanish Indians:

These people (of Yucatan) also made use of certain characters or letters, with which they wrote in their books their ancient affairs and their sciences, and with these and drawings and with certain signs in their drawings, they understood their affairs and made others understand them and taught them. We found a great number of characters in these books, and, as they contained nothing in which there was not to be seen superstition and lies of the devil, we burned them all, which they regretted to an amazing degree and caused them affliction. (S. K. Lothrop, *Treasures of Ancient America*, p. 124)

Professor Thomas Barthel, Director of the Folklore Institute of Tubingen University, told the 39th International Congress of

American Studies at Lima that he had succeeded in establishing 400 signs of an Inca writing. He was able to interpret the meaning of fifty of them and read twenty-four. It was not an alphabetical script. Peruvian and German scholars spoke of "attractive patterns and ornaments," which they thought were akin to writing.

Few scholars believed that the Peruvians used a form of writing until most recently when the theory of writing on "Pallares" (lima beans) was studied. There has been some study as to the possibility of a symbol representing a complete word without a reference to pronunciation. This is called "tokapus." Various colors were used in geometrical signs and symbols which were woven into textiles also. Secrecy seems to be a part of this system.

From the decipherment that has been completed to date, the number four was important to the Incas. Also, red was the royal color (Victor de la Jara, *Introduction el Estudio de la Escritura de los Inkas*, INIDE, 1975).

In a military sense, the concept of a "thousand" as employed in a military unit of organization and used in the Book of Mormon ninety-three times, is also used in the Elephantine papyri, an ancient document from Africa.

Studies have also been made which indicate a similarity in the origin of names between adjoining communities, some words having common roots, especially in the beginnings and endings of the names.

The custom of papponymy, or naming a child after an ancestor, was also frequent in the Book of Mormon and also in the Elephantine papyri.

When writing was done by hand, variations in colors were used for emphasis, and other reasons. Among the Cherokee Indians, white was used for peace or happiness, black for death, red for success, blue for defeat. Different colors of string in the use of the Quipu of ancient Peru were also a part of the message.

Artifacts of Writing in the New World

As the Indians changed from a hunting culture to an agricultural community, they erected more permanent homes, using stone as a medium. They carved it, painted it, and wrote on it. At first the writing was pictographic, more than ideographic, combining a number of pictographs into a single symbol which represented an idea. Eventually, the symbols no longer stood for idea, but for sounds, with these sounds put together to form words. And thus a phonetic alphabet came into being. Is this the Indian which migrated to this area from the Old World? If so, we would expect a reflection of the culture from the Old World in much of their culture including names, words, and writing. Some researchers believe that this is indeed the case.

Even those Indians who did not develop a written literature (as did the Aztec and the Maya of Mexico) used several kinds of notation and memory devices. A wooden box was used by the Ojibwa Indians of the western Great Lakes to store ceremonial eagle feathers. Pictograph designs on the cover served as reminders of the songs to be sung at the ceremonies. They could not be read by the uninitiated any more than Chinese can be read by an American without instruction.

Colonel Garrick Mallory and Dr. W. J. Hoffman, of the U. S. Bureau of Ethnology (1883), reported in a paper read before the Anthropology Society of Washington, D.C., that the Schoolcraft Report on the Ojibwa hieroglyphs was basically true, though exaggerated (as to the coloring of the birch-bark rolls, and to the concepts to be conveyed by the symbols thereon). This was published in *Powell's Seventh Annual Report of the Bureau of Ethnology*, page 156, paper of Hoffman on the "Mide-Wiwin or Grand Medicine Society of the Ojibwa." The Ojibwa were then located in northern Minnesota and Wisconsin.

Scholars know of three wooden tablets on Easter Island which contain writing. There have been five additional ancient tablets found at the Roman Catholic Mission in Tahiti, and an additional one which has been taken to San Francisco. Two others are housed in the National Museum at Santiago, Chile (Park J. Harrison, *Nature*, vol. 10, pp. 399,400). It is evident that many of these wooden tablets have been destroyed.

Adrian Chavez has discovered some writing on jade in Chichicastenago, Guatemala. Some of the signs are repeated several times, organized into vertical columns, and seemingly run from top to bottom, right to left. There are two types of signs, pictographs, and phonetic signs which determine pronunciation.

Byron Dix, Assistant Director of Research in the New England Antiquities Research Association of Vermont, has catalogued the discovery of fifty-one subterranean chambers discovered in Vermont alone, housing stones bearing organized markings.

Reports of finding ancient coins in America, bearing inscriptions, have become so numerous that Dr. Norman Totten, of the Boston Epigraphic Society, concludes that transoceanic crossings occurred before Columbus and even before Christ.

Besides numerous finds in the Southwest, a number of other artifacts have been unearthed in areas as widely diverse as Michigan, and the southern states. In 1966, for instance, Manfred Metcalf discovered a stone in Georgia which was called to the attention of the Columbus Museum of Arts and Crafts. Dr. Joseph Mahan, of the museum, worked on the Metcalf Stone and concluded that the inscriptions were produced by the Yuchi Indians, who maintained oral legends which told of transoceanic origins. Mahan's theory concerning a possible connection between the inscriptions on the stone and the Aegean linear script was sustained. Dr. Cyrus H. Gordon made further news by making the bold claim that the Phoenicians had at one time landed in Brazil and left inscriptions on what is now called the Parahyba Stone (Cyrus H. Gordon, *Before Columbus*, pp. 119-127).

Other areas of the South have produced written artifacts of pre-Columbian America. Stephen Peet, for example, has reported the finding of hieroglyphics on tablets near the banks of the Mississippi River, as well as the discovery of picture writing in Tennessee in the 1890s (Stephen Peet, *Prehistoric America*, 2 vols., pp. 44-45, 374).

Much publicity has been given to the Bat Creek Stone, found in Tennessee (London County). This engraved stone was discovered in 1885 during a Smithsonian mound exploration program under the direction of Professor Cyrus Thomas. The publicity came due to the fact that the irrepressible Dr. Gordon examined this stone as well, and suggested that the inscription was made between A.D. 70 and A.D. 135; and that the language on the stone could be linked to the Roman Empire during the first and second centuries A.D. (*Science 2*, May 1971, pp. 14-16).

Other southern artifacts include the Grave Creek and Wilson Tablets located in West Virginia, which have long been controversial objects containing characters considered to be Phoenician, Libyan, Celtiberic, and Runic (Western Reserve Historical Society Tracts, February 9, 1872).

The northern United States has likewise contributed evidence which supports the pre-Columbian written language theory.

At Newark, Ohio, a man by the name of Wyrick discovered two stones covered with old Hebrew inscriptions. M. E. Cornell has published an undated manuscript in Battle Creek, Michigan, which contains several drawings of caskets and tablets found in the vicinity of Wyman, Michigan. Many of these objects have inscriptions on them (J. Ralston Skinner, *Key to the Hebrews: Egyptian Mystery in the Sources of Measures*, 1875, p. 55). In addition, the January 1969 edition of *Science Digest* reports finding runic messages on stones discovered in Kensington, Minnesota; Poteau, Oklahoma; Bourne, Massachusetts; and the province of Nova Scotia.

This impressive, not to say convincing, catalog of North American finds may be equalled, if not surpassed, by a similar listing of artifacts uncovered in Central and South America. Hieroglyphics cut into stone were part of the Mayan culture, and inscriptions on the lintels of buildings in Chichen Itza, as well as the tablet at Palenque, and the stelae, or stone slabs of Tikal, explain certain calendrical and astronomical hieroglyphics (SEHA Newsletter, 112.0).

Lopez de Gomara gives an account of the books of the Indians of Nicaragua:

> They have books of paper and parchment, a hand in width and twelve hands in length, folded like bellows, on both sides of which they make known in blue, purple, and other colors, the memorable events which take place. (Lopez de Gomara, Historia General de last Indias, Historiators Primitivos de Indias, vols. XXII)

Father Francisco Ximenez indicated that in the province of Peten, the Spaniards found some books written in characters which resembled Hebrew characters and also those used by the Chinese (Francisco Fray Ximenez, Historia de la Provincia de San Vicente de Chiapa y Guatemala, vol. 1, p. 4).

Montezuma also referred to ancient records of his people:

> It is reported that when Cortes met Montezuma, the chief said, "Long time have we been informed by the writings of our ancestors . . ."

Sarmiento de Gamboa told of how the Inca, Pachacuti, consulted the historians of Tahuantinsuyo and had them paint the history of the Incas on big tablets and marked them with gold and deposited them in a special building (Pedro Sarmiento de Gamboa, History of the Incas [1575, in works issued by the Hakluyt Society, Series No. XXII, Cambridge, 1907]).*

Perhaps the most interesting discoveries in the search for pre-Columbia writings have been from the inscriptions on bowls found near Guadalajara, Mexico; also the artifacts found in Peru, which depict Mochica couriers carrying small sacks apparently containing incised lima beans painted with strange markings. Other painted pottery portrays men studying such

---

*As cited in Milton R. Hunter, Christ in Ancient America [Salt Lake City: Deseret Book, 1959].

beans. Scholars suppose that these persons were decoders, with the markings being some form of communication. The Peruvian Raphael Larco Hoyle saw in these symbols a close resemblance to Mayan glyphs.

Descriptions of Plates
Shown in Color Insert

Darius Persipolis Gold and Silver Plates

Trilingual, in duplicate on two gold and two silver plates; ten lines Old Persian, seven lines Elamite, and eight lines Akkadian sealed in a stone box. Apparently the author thought the message was important and needed to be preserved because the same message was found at Hamadan in one gold and one silver plate. The text again begins with a brief genealogy stating that Darius is the son of Hystospes and an Achaemenian.

The text then gives the boundaries of his kingdom which he states were given to him by Ahuramazda, the greatest of gods. He closes with a prayer that Ahuramazda will protect him and his royal house. Discovered in 1938.

Copper Plates with a Ring

The copper plates measure $3\frac{1}{2}'' \times 11''$ and were made circa 769 A.D. They are in the Sanskrit and Tamil languages and are identified as Parantaka Nedunjadaiyan. These 10 plates tell of H. Krishna Shastric Velvikudi grant of Nedunjadaiyan in the third year of his reign. Further reference is found in Epigraphia Indica Vol. XVII, pp. 291-309.

Gold Plate from Peru

The inscribed gold plate was found in Lamboyeque, northern Peru. It is a part of the Hugo Cohen Collection. It measures $8\frac{1}{4}'' \times 4\frac{1}{8}''$. It has writing symbols on it similar to the Cypriot language of Cyprus. It has been submitted to chemical tests at Ohio State University and at the University of Michigan and at two other laboratories. Opinions as to its authenticity have come from seven scholars. Both pro and con statements have been made concerning its ancient origin.

Darius Persipolis Gold and Silver Plates

Copper Plates with a Ring

Gold Plate from Peru

Writing Materials

For the purpose of recording events and communicating ideas, man naturally used materials which were most easily obtainable. Some of these materials were durable, and even the most crude writing could be preserved on materials such as stone, while the most sophisticated writing on materials such as papyrus would deteriorate. At times the portability of the materials was a factor; bark, leaves of trees, skins of animals, wooden lintels, adobe bricks, linen, shells, semi-precious stone, silk, stucco, bone, alabaster, ivory, murals, ceramics, clay cylinder seals, metals, and paper were used. Hard stone was probably one of the best means of preserving messages, although some noncorrosive metals such as gold have also been valuable to this extent. Eight thousand words in cuneiform script were carved in a stele about 2200 B.C. and now stands in the Louvre Museum in Paris. It tells of Hammurabi, king of Babylon, and was carved on black diorite. Other stones, such as the Rosetta Stone, exemplify the importance of this enduring type of writing.

Jade, rock crystal, and other precious stones were cut and used as seals, becoming additional methods of communication.

Clay was a most common material used by the Sumerians, Babylonians, and Assyrians. This material was formed into cylinders, as well as flat tablets. Thousands of these tablets have been found, and many are on display in many museums throughout the world. The shape of the character employed has given us the name of the writing—cuneiform, a term from the Latin cuneus, which means wedge. The writing is composed, therefore, of wedge-shaped characters.

Even walls of buildings were used as writing mediums. Anciently, wall spaces were used for the purpose of chronicling events. This custom has continued until the present day, and the ancient graffiti now being studied creates a great deal of interest.

The bark from a tree becomes the basis for the use of the word "book." Not only has the bark of the tree been used, but also the trunk and the leaves have been used for writing material. The term "codes," which is employed to name the ancient pre-Columbian books in America, is derived from the Latin form caudex, which means a trunk or stem of a tree. The codex was composed of folded sheets of paper.

Single tablets were sometimes prepared so that they could be reused. The surfaces were smooth and whitened with chalk or had gypsum or glaze applied to the surface. The writing was inscribed with charcoal or charcoal-ink. This could then be rubbed off with pumice stone or sponging.

Sometimes a single tablet would evolve into a set of tablets, consisting first of two, then later several — hinged together by means of cords or rings which passed through holes pierced in their margins, similar to a modern loose-leaf notebook. Normally these were made of wood, but some have been constructed from metal and ivory.

The use of leaves of trees for writing materials was popular in such countries as India where the talipot tree provides large and thick leaves. These leaves were dried, boiled, and dried again, and then smoothed with rollers or stones, then cut into oblong shapes for use. The simplest method of writing was to scratch or engrave characters upon the surface of a leaf by means of a sharp instrument, with a staining fluid rubbed into the engravings.

The inner bark of a lime tree was most suitable for writing surface, but bamboo and birch bark from India and North America were also used. Bamboo was especially adaptable to the Chinese writing since the bamboo strips lent themselves well to the vertical oriental syllables.

India also provides us with some beautiful gold plates with enameled writing, bound with copper rings (British Museum). Pottery was used as a writing material throughout the Mediterranean world, the Nile valley, and Greece. All types of messages were sent on potsherds, even tax receipts.

Linen was used in an earlier period by the Egyptians. Silk was a popular medium used in Mesopotamia in the early Mohammedan period before the use of papyrus. The origin of silk writing had its beginning in China.

It is not surprising that the skins of animals were often used as writing material, with the hair side being rubbed smooth in preparation for writing. Such skins were used in Egypt as early as 2000 B.C. The earliest known specimen is in the British Museum and dated 2000 B.C.

A tall water plant on the banks of the Nile provided an almost revolutionary writing material. Papyrus then became the principle writing material of the ancient world. Strips of the stem of this plant were prepared by squeezing, beating, pressing, and drying. They were polished with an ivory or shell burnisher. By gluing they could make a roll of considerable length. Unfortunately, of all possible materials for permanent use, papyrus is among the worst. The effect of time makes it brittle and dry, and with handling it crumples into dust.

The materials destined to take the place of all of the aforementioned medium is paper. Invented in China about A.D. 105, its use is now worldwide. Made from various products, but principally from wood pulp, paper has revolutionized the printing and writing industry.

The earliest form of a writing instrument was probably a pointed flint flake or bone. As civilization developed, harder instruments were used. With the cuneiform script, a blunt punch-like form for impressing the wedge-shaped characters was used. Later, a harder instrument called a stylus was used for embossing. Brushes, quill pens, circular discus of lead, erasers, and various forms of inks were utilized. In modern times printer's ink combined with ball-point and felt-tipped pens have made writing much easier.

All of the advanced cultures of ancient Mexico used some form of writing and writing material. Some have even reported the use of an encyclopedia called *Teoamextili*. This was a divine book compiled about A.D. 600.

Paper was also a popular medium for writing in ancient America. Montezuma reportedly kept his revenue records on books which were made of a type of paper called *amatl*, and the Toltecs, Mixtecs, and Zapotecs were also known to have had paper and writing (Victor Wolfgang Von Hagen, *The Ancient Sun Kingdoms of the Americas*, p. 38).

At the turn of the century some papyri was found at Aswan and has become known as the Elephantine papyri. The translation of the documents tells of a group of Jewish soldiers who left Jerusalem to protect the Persian interests in South Egypt. Since the Book of Mormon contains a record of an expedition at approximately the same time, we would expect some parallels of culture and language in these two groups. As the records unfold, we find that both people are interested in building a temple soon after they arrive at their destination. Not only do the Elephantine documents support the idea of building the temple, they also agree with the Book of Mormon as to the name for the temple and the specific name for deity.

The Peruvian quipu (kee-pu) is a series of knotted strings assembled together to transmit a message. Various colors of strings were used. Because communication was accomplished, it was thought by some to be a form of writing. For the purpose of record keeping, each knot represented a digit, the placement of the knot on the string, another meaning. The color added another dimension. This system had wide distribution in the Americas and occurs as well in China and adjoining sections of the Old World.

Attached to the regular strings were subordinate strings which acted as an appendage or footnote.

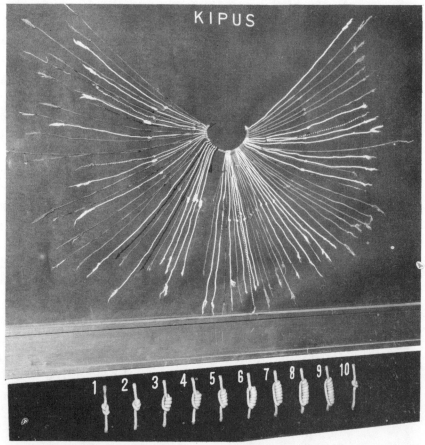

The Quipus (Kipus), a knot system of mathematics used by the ancient Peruvians

It is interesting to note that one writer observed that the use of the quipu was widespread in Polynesia and Micronesia (J. M. Brown, *The Riddle of the Pacific*, p. 265).

Turner (1861) said that Samoans used a knotted cord for remembering ideas. Friederici (1929) reported a similar use with Maoris and the Marquesas group, as well as Hawaii and Rarotonga. Denger (1949) spoke of the Maoris, and the Polynesians used a form of the quipu, all these uses emphasize the belief that the Polynesians had migrated from South America (Thor Heyerdahl, *American Indians in the Pacific*, p. 639).

In 1680 the Pueblo Indians communicated the number of days before their great uprising against the Spaniards by means of a knotted string, and some of their descendants kept personal calendars by the same means. *Boas*, Bulletin, American Museum of Natural History XV, 1901, shows similar use of knots in the Eskimo life.

Wampum strings (similar to quipu) were used by the Delawares as memory devices. The Catawba Indians used knots to send messages (D. S. Brown, *The Catawba Indians*, p. 98).

The tax gatherers of Hawaii kept accurate records by means of knotted string (Albert P. Taylor, *Under Hawaiian Skies*, p. 246). This is also true of other Polynesian islands (*Ibid.*, p. 639).

Governor James Moore of South Carolina sent knots to all the Indians thereabouts for every town to send in ten skins. The skins were a tribute demand by the colony, and the cord with knots was the white man's way of conveying the idea of numbers to the Indians.

Proceedings of the Tenth Pacific Science Congress in Honolulu, Hawaii, in 1961, unanimously accepted the resolution that not only southeastern Asia, but also South America were major origins for the peoples and cultures of the Pacific Islands. The possibility of the idea of the quipu coming from South America or vice versa is certainly a consideration.

Dr. Peter Matthews and Doris Reents, of Harvard University and the University of Texas respectively, have confirmed that the ostracon found at El Mirador, Guatemala, was an example of genuine writing. This makes it the earliest example of writing found in the Mayan world.

Survey of Mesoamerican Codices

Pictorial glyphic codices on amatl (bark), paper and skins were used through Mesoamerica in ancient times, and over 400 examples or fragments of examples have survived to the present day. Of these 400, sixteen are generally considered unquestionably pre-Columbian, so they hold a special interest. The other codices were written after the contact period, but they were done according to native tradition and languages, so they may be considered partly pre-Columbian in content. The extant codices date from the 16th century. By the end of the 16th century, the Indians throughout Mesoamerica were literate and the use of codices for communication purposes all but disappeared.

The origin or antiquity of the use of the codices is undetermined. The practice was distributed throughout the region from Central Mexico to Nicaragua. The codex tradition was especially strong in the Maya region and among the Mixtec-Zapotec peoples of western Oaxaca. Recently three ancient codices dating from the early classic Maya period have been recovered archaeologically to date, two of them at Mirador in southeastern Mexico, and one at the Maya site of Altun Ha in Belize. All three codices, although too badly decayed to be deciphered or even separated, are dated to about A.D. 450. So by that time, the codical tradition was firmly entrenched in nuclear America.

At the time of the Spanish Conquest there were literally thousands of codices in collections throughout the Aztec, Mixtec, and Maya areas of Mesoamerica. Unfortunately, only sixteen pre-Columbian documents have survived to the present day.

The Museo de America in Madrid displayed the Mayan Madrid Codex written on paper made from the bark of the wild fig tree. It is in two segments totaling about 680 centimeters in length. Originally, it came from the Yucatan Peninsula and contains a ritual calendar the Mayas used for divination. It has specific sections devoted to various occupations, such as hunting, beekeeping, weaving, etc.

Two important codices from the Mixtec-Puebla area were sent to Europe by Cortez in 1519. They eventually ended up in the Vatican Library where this author was graciously allowed to examine them. The Codex Borgia, named after the famous Italian family, is an exquisite work of art, as well as an important literary document. Painted on skins, it consists of thirty-nine leaves 27 centimeters square, written on both sides, and joined together to form a continuous screenfold over a thousand centimeters long.

The codex is a 260-day ritual calendar that was used in religious ceremonies and divination. Codex Vaticanus 3773, commonly called Vaticanus B, is much smaller than the Borgia, although very similar in content.

Codex Vaticanus 3773
Vatican Library, Rome

A number of the Mexican codices are now in the Bibliotheque Nationale in Paris. There this author was permitted to see the Mayan Codex Paris from Yucatan, a small fragment consisting of eleven pages from a much longer original. At the same time I saw the Aztec Codex Borbonicus and the Tonalamatl Aubin, both from Central Mexico.

After the contact period, the Codices show a marked deterioration in both style and content. The art form gradually assumed more and more European influence as the 1500s progressed, so the better examples are those that date closest to the conquest. Other codices of great value are undoubtedly still in the possession of native villages in Mexico and Guatemala. As the process of education in those countries continues, there will probably be more codices coming to light. The forms of codices are:

1. The *tira*. A long strip either folded or rolled like a scroll.
2. The *screenfold* or "accordian" book, often framed in wood.
3. The *liezo*, like a large painted canvas, used primarily for maps and boundary designations.

Of these, the screenfold books are the most famous and generally the best preserved. After the conquest, the codices appeared on European paper, the liezos on European cloth. Most of the codices have only begun to be studied. Their dates, their styles, and content are generally only superficially known. The four hundred-plus codices with significant pre-Columbian content can be categorized as follows:

Pre-conquest

There are sixteen known examples, not counting the badly decayed fragments uncovered archaeologically in the last decade.

The sixteen pre-Columbian codices are generally histories, genealogies, and ritual or divinatory almanacs. The four or perhaps five Mayan and Mixtec codices are the most famous groups. Of these, the Codex Dresden is the best preserved, the most beautiful artistically, and the most widely studied. It is generally considered the finest example of pre-Columbian Mesoamerican art.

Besides the Codex Dresden, the other outstanding codices, both for artistic style and state of preservation, are the Codex Borgia, the Codex Vaticanus 3773 in the Vatican Library, the Codex Nuttall in the British Museum, and the Codex Madrid located in the Museum de America, Madrid.

Post-conquest

Sixteenth century copies of pre-conquest works. These were often made at the request of a Spanish officer or clergyman who took an interest in Indian antiquities.

De novo works, created during the Colonial period, but firmly in the native tradition. Codices "commissioned" by the Spaniards.

Native Colonial Creations

These were histories of pre-Columbian works. Some were genealogies written to perpetuate memory of the ancient lines for a native prince's ancestors. These native documents were often written at great personal hazard to the author, since codices in general were suspected, and the only ones officially tolerated by the Spanish ecclesiastical authorities were those created specifically for Spanish antiquarians.

Mixed Colonial

These are the bulk of the surviving codices. They are a degenerate form, getting gradually poorer and more Europeanized toward the end of the 16th century. They were generally used as a means of communication for colonial business matters in the days before colonial officials in the native villages could read and write Spanish. These documents are governmental records, economic reports, tribute lists, land titles, etc.

Bernal Diaz saw piles of books near the Totonac city-state of Cempoala:

> Then we came on some towns . . . [and] found idol houses . . . and paper books doubled together in folds like Spanish cloth . . .
> Later Bernal Diaz del Castillo accompanied Cortes and looked at the stored treasures of this tribute-state and into where Montezuma 'kept the accounts of all the revenue . . . in his books which were made of paper which they call *amatl* and he had a great house full of these books. (Victor Wolfgang von Hagen, *The Ancient Sun Kingdoms of the Americas*, pp. 38, 183)

THE SIXTEEN PRE-COLUMBIAN MESOAMERICAN CODICES

Name	Provenience/Cultural Identification	Description	Content	Actual Location
1. Tonalamatl Aubin	Tlaxcala? Central Mexico	Native paper screenfold, 18 leaves, 24 × 27 cm.	Ritual-calendrical divinatory almanac, patron deities	Bibliotheque Nationale Paris
2. Codex Borbonicus	Tenochtitlan-Aztec Central Mexico	Native paper screenfold, 36 × 39 cm.	Ritual-calendrical 260-day divinatory almanac — excellent pictorial detail	Bibliotheque de L' Assemblee Nationale Francaise, Paris Palais Bourbon
3. Codex Borgia	(?) Puebla-Tlaxcala-Western Oaxaca	Skin screenfold, perhaps the most beautiful of all codices, 39 leaves, 27 × 27 cm., 1034 cm. 1	Ritual-calendrical 260-day ritual calendar	Biblioteca Apostolica Vaticana, Rome
4. Codex Cospi	(?) Puebla-Tlaxcala-Western Oaxaca	Skin screenfold, 20 leaves	Ritual-calendrical, 18 × 18 cm., 364 cm. long	Biblioteca Universitaria, Bologna
5. Codex Fejervary-Mayer	(?) Western Oaxaca	Skin screenfold, 23 leaves, 17 × 17 cm., 385 cm. long	Ritual-calendrical divinatory almanac	Free Public Museums Liverpool

THE SIXTEEN PRE-COLUMBIAN MESOAMERICAN CODICES
(continued)

Name	Provenience/Cultural Identification	Description	Content	Actual Location
6. Codex Laud	(?) Western Oaxaca	Skin screenfold, 24 leaves, 16 × 16 cm., 400 cm. long	Ritual-calendrical	Bodleian Library, Oxford
7. Codex Vaticanus B (Vaticanus 3773)	(?) Western Oaxaca	Skin, 49 leaves, 13 × 15 cm., 735 cm. long	Ritual-calendrical 260-day ritual almanac	Biblioteca Apostolica Vaticana, Rome
8. Aubin Manuscript No. 20	Mixtec, Western Oaxaca	Skin, 51 × 91 cm.	Ritual-calendrical	Bibliotheque Nationale, Paris
9. Codex Becker No. 1	Tututepec, Western Oaxaca Mixtec	Skin screenfold, 16 leaves, 296.4 cm. long	Historical-life and history of Ruler 8 Deer from 1047-1068 A.D.	Museum fur Volkerkunde, Vienna
10. Codex Bodley	Mixtec, Western Oaxaca	Skin screenfold, 23 leaves	Historical-genealogical, contains historical data back to 692 A.D.	Bodleian Library, Oxford
11. Codice Colombino	Tututepec, Western Oaxaca Mixtec	Skin screenfold, 24 leaves, 606 cm. long	Historical-history of ruler 8 Deer from 1028 to 1048 A.D.	Museo Nacional de Antropologia, Mexico City

THE SIXTEEN PRE-COLUMBIAN MESOAMERICAN CODICES
(continued)

Name	Provenience/Cultural Identification	Description	Content	Actual Location
12. Codex Nuttall	Mixtec, Western Oaxaca	Skin screenfold, 47 leaves, one of the best preserved best known codices	Historical-genealogical history between 9th and 14th centuries	British Museum Add. Mss. 39671
13. Codex Vienna	Mixtec, Western Oaxaca sent by Cortes to Charles V in 1519	Skin, 52 leaves	Ritual-calendrical mythological genealogies	National Bibliothek Vienna Collection CVM-1
14. Codex Dresden	Lowland Maya	Amatl paper screenfold, 39 leaves, the best preserved, most famous Maya codex	Divinatory almanacs, astronomical calculations, glyphic texts	Sachsische Landes Bibliothek, Dresden
15. Codex Madred (Codex Tro-Cortesiano)	Lowland Maya	Amatl paper screenfold, 56 leaves, 682 cm. long, 2 segments	Ritual-calendrical divination, hunting, beekeeping, weaving, etc.	Museo de America, Madrid
16. Codex Paris	Lowland Maya	Amatl paper screenfold, 11 leaves, 145 cm. long	Ritual-calendrical prophecies, divinatory almanac	Bibliotheque Nationale, Paris #386

Furthermore, a type of paper has been found which dates back to the pre-Columbian period in Mexican history, and is currently on display in the anthropological museum in Mexico City. In 1968, Thomas Stuart Ferguson discovered a scroll of paper-like material with linked characters inscribed on it. In his book, *The First Americans* (n.d.), G. H. S. Bushnell discusses the findings of manuscripts painted on bark cloth, which was then sized with lime and folded like a screen. These manuscripts contain bar and dot numerals as well as other glyphs. These rare codices on display in major museums have been declared to be a very stylized form of writing. Certain pictographic representations in the New World Codex Vaticanus (one of the few remaining New World manuscripts) have been interpreted as representing the characters of Adam, Eve, Cain, Abel, and a serpent.

Roller-Stamp (Cylinder) Writing

A brief article by David H. Kelley in the July 1966 issue of *American Antiquity* is of interest to students of the Book of Mormon. It reports the finding of a roller stamp (or cylinder seal, as Dr. Kelly calls it) bearing three lines of apparent writing, in a deposit of Olmec material at Tlatilco in the Valley of Mexico. The following is an abstract of the article:

> The roller stamp was found on the surface of the brick works at Tlatilco in 1948 by Frederick A. Peterson. It was encased in a large lump of clay detached by the workers. Inside the lump was a type "D" figurine, identifying the stamp as belonging to the "Olmec" horizon (i.e., c. 1000-500 B.C.).
>
> The stamp is 8.5 cm. long and 3.5 cm. in diameter. It has three registers one of which is partly missing. All three registers carry sequences of arbitrary symbols which Dr. Kelley believes belong to a hitherto unknown writing system.

This is one of the first clear-cut evidences of writing on cylinder seals from the Valley of Mexico, dating back to pre-Aztec times. Comparison with other early Mesoamerican examples reveals a form unlike any other known. Very few clear-cut

Tlatilco Cylinder Seal

examples of "Pre-classic" (Book of Mormon period) writing is known and all are vastly different from the writing on the Tlatilco stamp. All other ancient Mesoamerican scripts make use of some form of the head. These heads face to the right in the pre-classic examples and the left in later ones. The complete absence of heads in this script differentiates it from all other known Mesoamerican writing systems.

This newly reported find of a possible early linear script in Mesoamerica may give but a glimpse of what future excavations may unearth.

Before 3000 B.C., seals had progressed from button to stamp shape (flat with handles like our rubber stamps) and then to a cylindrical form so they could be rolled. The carvings on the seals passed through a pictorial stage to one in which only symbols of words were used. Some say this was the beginning of printed writing.

Writing on Metal Plates

Plates of metal were employed by the Greeks as far back as 500 B.C. Lead plates were used by both the Greeks and Romans. Bronze tablets were also popular with these people, especially for more official documents, such as the bronze treaty tablets in the Athens Archaeological Museum. During the reign of Emperor Vespasian, it is estimated there were 3,000 tablets of bronze documents which were burned. Certain military tablets had two square plates hinged together with rings. The plates were then securely fastened together by a wire being passed through holes drilled in the rim and bound round them. Plutarch mentions a golden book in the treasury of the Sicyonians of Delphi (Quast—Conviv. v., pp. 2-10). Of course, the durability of a metal such as gold cannot be overemphasized. If a person would wish for a record to endure without oxidation, gold would be a perfect metal for this.

In the Bible it is recorded that ancient writings were inscribed on gold (Exodus 28:36; 39:30).

Although the Roman laws were supposed to have been kept in the capitol and inscribed in bronze, inscriptions on metal flourished mainly in India and parts of Southeast Asia. The earliest inscribed copper plates come from the Indus Valley (ca. 2800 B.C.) but since we cannot read the script we are ignorant of their exact purpose. In historical times it was common practice for Indian kings, subordinate rulers, or persons of exceptional wealth and standing to make grants of land and have the gift recorded on copper-plate charters which served the recipients as title deeds. Since the text of the actual grant is usually preceded by genealogical and personal accounts concerning the donor, copper plates were important historical documents. The plates were fashioned with hammer and brazier, the engraving was done from a draft (on birch bark, cotton, or palm leaf), or the text was written directly onto the surface of the plate for the engraver to follow. Some plates were oblong or square, either single, or meant to fit into each other for protection of the scripts, but in most cases they followed the already familiar shape of the palm leaf and were strung together by a ring which bore the donor's seal.

Old plates would sometimes be re-used by hammering out the original inscription; forgers could thus replace the name of the rightful beneficiary. Normally owners would take great care to preserve their plates and if the grant was made to a religious institution the text was, as an additional precaution, often copied on the temple wall. A good example is the great temple of Tanjore, south of Madras, India. The lower parts of its walls were covered with inscriptions with datings from various periods, using a variety of different scripts. Not all surviving copper plates were documents. Jain, Buddhist, and Hindu scriptures have been immortalized in this fashion. Brass was used, too, though less frequently.

Lead, being rather a soft metal, was fairly popular throughout the ancient world. It can easily be beaten into thin sheets, inscribed and then rolled up for storage. Pliny and Pausanias both make references to lead sheets used for writing. Lead was also used by the Hittites, and the Mandaens. A gnostic sect speaking an Aramaic dialect used inscribed lead amulets from about the 6th century A.D. Tin was sometimes used in Malaysia but it seems mainly as a substitute for silver. Iron presents technological difficulties as it has to be soft enough for engraving and also rustproof to survive. The famous Iron Pillar of Delhi with an inscription dating from the 4th century A.D. is a notable exception whose uniqueness for the place and period has provoked a good deal of speculation. Reference has already been made to inscribed weapons. Steel swords from India and from the Islamic world are frequently inscribed with the names of their owners, verses from the Qur'an, or appropriate passages from literature.

This leaves the precious metals, gold and silver, which were repeatedly used in many ancient civilizations. *Their use was determined usually by a desire to stress the value of a religious text, to gain special merit by commissioning so expensive a 'book,' to show proper respect for the position of the person to whom a letter or message was addressed, or simply to draw attention to one's own wealth and standing.* Some of the most interesting examples are perhaps two beaten gold sheets from Burma (5th century A.D.) inscribed with a famous Pali verse. They were found in 1896, inside a brick, no doubt the foundation stone of a Buddhist structure. In Sri Lanka, the entire Buddhist canon was, according to tradition, written on gold plates in 88 B.C. and, as late as the 19th century, Southeast Asian princes would at times still have their letters written on thin sheets of pure gold (Albertine Gaur, *Writing Materials of the East*).

In 1968 the author was viewing a private pre-Columbian artifact collection in Lima, Peru. Hanging on the wall was a thin gold plaque (found in the Lambayeque area) bearing an interesting embossed design which, upon closer examination, revealed eight distinct symbols. This plate has since been examined by several scholars throughout the United States and has undergone neutron, X-ray, and spectographic analysis to determine its composition. It was found to be ninety percent gold. Although some have questioned its authenticity, others are less skeptical, and studies are still going on to determine its value. In a study by Luige Palma Cresnola, a comparison of the markings from this plate with certain characters from an ancient Old World cyprite text reveals striking similarities.

In January 1970, the author learned of the existence of seven inscribed metal plates belonging to a Catholic priest in Ecuador, who for many years has been collecting artifacts from Indians in surrounding areas. The author visited this gentleman shortly after learning of his collection and secured photographs of the plates. Six were of copper and one of an alloy of copper, gold, and zinc or tin. Tests and analyses to establish the authenticity or invalidity of these plates will take many months, or even years.

A discovery of pre-historic copper sheets was reported in Dunklin County, Missouri. They seemed to represent double eagles, with similarities found in the Mexican and Central American cultures. Peabody Institute agreed that this was a connecting link between the Mexican central peoples and the mound builders of the Mississippi (Louis Houck, *A History of Missouri*, vol. 1, pp. 395-403).

No more can critics of the Book of Mormon deny that ancient records were kept on metal plates. Modern discoveries

In the Museum of the American Indian in New York is found this gold disk. It is from the northern part of Peru and is thought to date to approximately 800 B.C. Inscriptions embossed on this disk have been recognized as a calendar system.

Gold plate from Peru with eight distinct writing symbols.

Copper Plates from Cuenea, Ecuador

now support the idea that writing on metal was a very common ancient practice in both the Old World and the New World.

References to metal plates are found even in classical literature. Plutarch mentions finding a bronze writing tablet at his feet when a local spring boiled up (Plutarchus, *Quaestiones convivales*, 5.2). Inscribed plates made of lead, gold, silver, and copper have also been found in relative abundance in the Old World since 1830.

During archaeological diggings in Franzfeld, South Russia, in 1898, Jacob Schaub's sons found twelve small gold metal plates in a hill. On the plates the twelve months were represented by forms of animals (Rev. P. Conrad Killer, *The German Colonies in South Russia, 1804-1904*, p. 248).

Marshall Howard Saville reported findings of thin gold plates in Mexico:

> Padre Gay mentions that the Mixtecan Indians "sold to some European antiquarians, very thin plates of gold, evidently worked with the hammer, which their ancestors had been able to preserve, and on which were engraved ancient hieroglyphs." (Marshall Howard Saville, *The Goldsmith's Art in Ancient Mexico*, p. 175)

Peter De Roo wrote of an ancient book belonging to the Otomi Indians:

> The Indian narrated to him how, long ago the Otomis were in possession of a book, handed down from father to son and guarded by persons of importance, whose duty it was to explain it. Each page of that book had two columns, and between these columns were paintings which represented Christ crucified, whose features wore the expression of sadness; and such is the God who reigns, they said. For the sake of reverence, they did not turn the leaves with their hands, but with a tiny stick kept along with the book for the purpose. The friar having asked the Indian what the contents of the volume were and its teachings, the old man could not give the details, but said that, were it in existence yet, it would be evident that the teachings of that book and the preaching of the friar were one and the same. But the venerable heirloom had perished in the ground, where its guardians had buried it. (Peter De Roo, *America Before Columbus*, pp. 224, 225)

Concerning the legend of the Golden Book of the Maya, Verrill remarked:

> According to tradition a complete history of the Mayas was recorded in the Golden Book of the Mayas which, if it probably did, was so carefully hidden to prevent it from falling into the hands of the Spaniards that it never has been found. (Hyatt Verrill, *America's Ancient Civilizations*, p. 23)

Tradition indicates the *Golden Books of the Mayas* were fifty-two golden plates threaded on gold bars and engraved with characters which tell the entire history of the Mayan people. Whether or not such records ever existed, or whether they were found and melted down to bullion by the Spanish, or whether (as tradition declares) they were hidden by the Mayan priests and never have been found, no one really knows (*Ibid.*, p. 42).
Researchers Rivero and Tschudi also added:

> The Ancient Peruvians possessed two kinds of writing: the one and surely the most ancient consisted of certain hieroglyphic characters; the other of knots made with strings of various colors. The hieroglyphs, very different from the Mexican ones, were sculptured in stone or engraved on metal. (Mariano Eduardo de Rivero and Dr. Juan Diego de Tschudi, *Antiquedodes Pervanos*, p. 101)

When Sir Francis Drake sailed into San Francisco Bay in the 1580s, he claimed the territory for England and erected a bronze plaque as a witness. The replica of this plate is displayed in the Bancroft Library, Berkeley, California. During the 1950s the Peabody Museum participated in a project at Chichen Itza on the Yucatan Peninsula. Alfred Tozzer directed a team which dredged the sacred well (cenote) at this site, and found a number of embossed gold discs among the offerings which had been thrown into the sacrificial well. One of these, in particular, bears an inscription in Mayan glyphs around the edge of the disc. It is currently on display in the Peabody Museum at Harvard University. This is an excellent example of writing on metal — one which scholars accept as genuine, insofar as the New World is concerned.

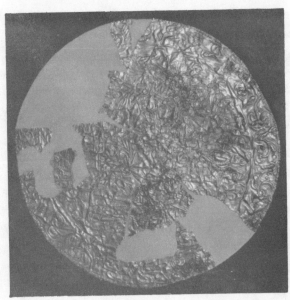

One of the best-known examples of ancient writing on metal in the New World comes from the ancient sacrificial well or Cenote in Chichen Itza on the Yucatan Peninsula in Mexico. When the crew from Peabody Museum at Harvard University began the dredging of the well, they found a number of embossed gold discs, among which was one which bore Mayan inscriptions. This well dates back into the cultures before Columbus, and the gold disc is now displayed in the Peabody Museum at Harvard University.

J. Eric Thompson, noted hieroglyphic researcher, wrote of hieroglyphic inscriptions found in Middle America on bone, shell, semiprecious stone, and very rarely on metal (J. Eric Thompson, *Handbook of Middle American Indian*, vol. 3, p. 634). Juan de Torquemada discusses the ancient Toltecs writing:

> And they say as well that they (the Toltecs) had knowledge of how the world was going to end again by consummation of fire, and this should be the same as that which they tell of the ancients, who wrote many things in two columns, one of metal and the other of brick or stone, so that if a fire came the column of brick would remain intact. (Juan de Torquemada, Libro I, Capitulo XIV, *Monarquia Indiana*, first ed., 1615)

As the author viewed the several parallels that were present in the displays at the Archaeological Museum in Cairo, such as the wheeled toys, tweezers, masks over mummies, and fish-hooks, he noticed that the King Tut's gold sarcophagus contained writing on that metal.

In the National Museum in Jerusalem, Mier Meyer, director of public affairs, showed us a silver leaf with letters in a square script. It was identified as Roman-Byzantine.

In the city of Jerusalem at Sade and Fayez Barakat & Sons, on David Street, the author viewed several bronze stamps bearing ancient writing symbols. He also saw writing on an ancient gold amulet.

Following is a plate known as Orphic Plate #293 in one identification from the Stathatos collection.

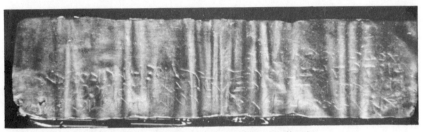

Orphic Plate #293 from the Stathatos Collection

I am dry with thirst and perish; therefore give me to drink from the everflowing spring at the right of the cypress tree (?). Who are you? Whose child are you? I am son of Earth and Starry Sky.

The Orphic religion was a Greek movement centered around the God Orpheus, the lyrist. The religion began in ancient Greece, then spread throughout the Mediterranean world at about 400 B.C. to A.D. 200. The major source of information comes from nine gold plates found in burials in Crete and Italy. The plates were buried with the dead and contained information on what the dead needed to do in order to make the transition to afterlife.

Of the nine plates discovered, two are in the British Museum, four are in a museum in Naples, and three are in Athens. One of the three from Athens is depicted here. They came from Eleuthernai in Crete, and date from the second century B.C.

On February 13, 1965, *The London Illustrated News* carried an exciting article with pictures telling of the discovery of some very thin gold plates—almost as thin as gold leaf, bearing ancient inscriptions.

This discovery was made in Italy, at the site of an ancient port city of Pyrgi, on the coast of the Tyrrhenian Sea, about thirty miles north of Rome.

The ancient town dates back to five centuries before Christ, and is located in what was once called the nation of Etruria.

Archaeologists have been studying this site since 1956, under the direction of the Institute of Etrusocology and Italic Antiquities of the University of Rome.

Massimo Pallottino, director of the expedition working on the site, reports the discovery of two Etruscan temples, as well as many pieces of painted terra-cotta relief, statues, slabs with geometric motifs, pottery, and a vast number of silver coins.

But the most unusual discovery of all came when the archaeologists found three thin rectangular sheets of gold, all about the same size—7½ inches long and 5½ inches wide. On one side of each sheet were three holes, with rivets still in place, indicating they had been fastened either to each other or to some other object, possibly making them into a book.

All three bore engraved inscriptions, one of them in the Phoenician language, the other two in ancient Etruscan. All have been translated, and are tributes to a pagan goddess, expressing gratitude for her protection.

Pallottino indicates that the inscriptions can be securely dated to about 500 B.C., or the first years of the fifth century. Pyrgi was an ancient shrine on the coast of Italy. The Phoenician writing is Punic which flourished only a few miles from Jerusalem in Lehi's days.

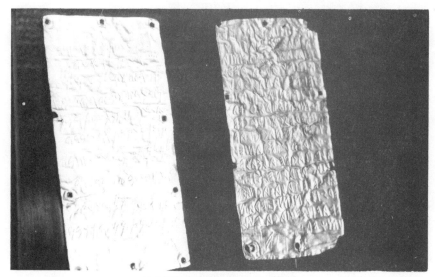

Gold Plates Discovered in Italy

This is the sixty-third location in which archaeologists have found metal plates, most of which have contained engravings of ancient vintage.

With more than ordinary interest we note that Pallottino suggested their dating at 500 B.C., which is so near to the time when Lehi left Palestine for his voyage to America.

The Pyrgi gold plates and some Pyrgi bronze plates, along with the Segni bronze plate, plus about thirty other various metal objects with writing on them, are found in the National Museum of Villa Giulia in the Piazza de Villa Giulia 9, Rome.

The National Museum of Villa Giulia 9, in Rome houses

1. The three gold plates of Pyrgi
2. The bronze plates of Pyrgi
3. The Seini bronze plate
4. Thirty various objects bearing inscriptions.

Seven bronze tablets were discovered in 1444 at Iguvium (Gubbio), Italy. They are now located in the Palazzo dei Consoli where the author viewed them. Written in the Umbrian dialect, each of the seven plates, with the exception of III and IV, are inscribed on both sides.

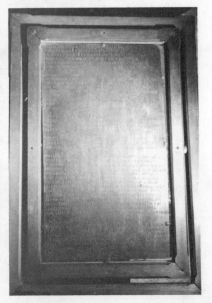

The Bronze Tablets at Gubbio, Italy

The tablets contain instructions for the religious ceremonies of a college of priests known as the Atiedian Brothers
who flourished in Iguvium during the period of the Roman
Republic. The tablets do not all date from the same time, but
the most recent date is from the first century B.C.

They are called the "Tavole Eugubine," and they are located in the

> Museum and Picture Gallery
> Palazzo dei Consoli
> Piazza della Signoria
> Gubbio, Umbria, Italy.

The plates of Darius were found in Persia and archaeologists have placed them at about 500 B.C. These records were
also engraved, one being of silver, the other being of gold. Each
told of the works of King Darius, who cast Daniel into the lions'
den.

One of the most interesting aspects of the study of the
plates of Darius is that they were found in a stone box constructed somewhat as Joseph Smith described the box in which
the Book of Mormon plates were found.

But still another discovery has been made: the plates of
Sargon, from Assyria, also engraved upon metal, were found
buried in a stone box of similar description.

Other metal records which have been unearthed have
been of various metals, such as gold, silver, bronze, brass, copper,
and even tin. Some were engraved, others were not. Some bore
court records, while yet others told of tribute to Pagan gods and
goddesses of ancient religions; yet others were personal inscriptions on very small plates used as ornaments.

Recent discoveries have proven fully that metal was not
only an excellent method and means of preserving valuable information, but a well-established custom. Such records were most
voluminous.

The Dead Sea Scrolls support this method strongly, for one
of them was copper, as have other scrolls of the same period,
these dating to about 200 B.C.

Plates of Darius found in Persepolis
Dating 518 B.C. to 515 B.C.

The Plates of Darius I, ruler of Persia from 518-515 B.C., are the closest parallel to the Book of Mormon plates yet discovered. Two tablets, one of gold and one of silver, were placed in each box buried at the four corners of his palace. They describe the boundaries of his kingdom, praise Ahuramazda, "the greatest of all the gods," and pray protection upon Darius "and my royal house." They were discovered by an archaeological team in 1938. (National Archaeological Museum, Tehran, Iran)

Ten lines of Old Persian, seven lines of Elamite, and eight lines of Akkadian were found on the plates. The same message was also found at Hamadan. The text begins with a genealogy stating that Darius is the son of Hystospes and an Achaemenian.

A curious love charm found in Tomb 2 at Ballana was written in Barbaric Greek on a piece of gold foil with a stylus, and then rolled up and tossed into the tomb (Edward Bacon, ed, *Vanished Civilizations of the Ancient World*, p. 77).

Six metal plates of Sargon II were deposited in the foundation stone of the Assyrian palace Khorsabad built by the king himself. They were placed in a chest somewhere between 714-705 B.C. The plates were found in 1853 by Victor Place.

The materials used in making the plates were, according to Olmstead, gold, silver, copper, lead, alabaster, and tin.

Copper Scroll from Qumran located in Amman, Jordan

Among the records discovered at Qumran in 1952 were two rolled copper scrolls, once riveted together but now separated. The brittle oxidized copper, dating from the second century B.C., was carefully sawed into longitudinal strips in Manchester, England, and deciphered. They catalogue a still-buried treasure of gold, silver, coins, earthen and metal vessels, and carious offerings worth several million dollars by today's price. (National Museum, Amman, Jordan)

However, the chest and two of the tablets, those of lead and alabaster, were lost when a ship carrying them sank on May 23, 1855, in the Tigris River. The inscriptions on the plates were made in cuneiform, and a brief summary of their translation follows:

> King Sargon II introduces himself, states that the gods Assur and Marduk have given him what he has, tells of some of his accomplishments, and ends with a prayer that whosoever destroys his works or name will have his own name and his seed destroyed from off the land; but that whatsoever restores its ruins be heard in prayer.

(The author viewed the Sargon gold plate in the Musee de Louvre in Paris, France.)

The Sargon II plate is of gold, one of six found in a chest buried between 714-705 B.C. in Khorsabad, in the foundations of Sargon's palace in ancient Assyria. The other five plates were made of silver, lead, tin, alabaster, and copper. After the discovery in 1854, two of the plates sank with their ship in the Tigris in 1855; the remaining four were brought to Paris. The cuneiform inscription announces that Assur and Marduk (gods of Assyria) gave Sargon II his kingdom, lists some of his accomplishments, and invokes a curse on anyone who attacks his works or reputation. (The Louvre, Paris)

Examples of writing on moulded animals were also found. Shown is an example in the National Museum of Villa Guilia in Rome, Italy.

In addition to the Pyrgi gold plates of Italy, the stone boxes and the silver and gold plates of Darius, the Orphic gold plates of Greece and the copper scrolls from the Qumran community, hundreds of others have been studied. In the archaeological museum at Athens are fragments of completed bronze, lead, and copper plates containing treaties, military and civil announcements, as well as temple dedications. In Italy not only did they write on plates, but the metal pedestals of statues, metal animals, metal rings, crowns, etc., bore ancient engraved inscriptions. In the British Museum the ancient writings from India in the Pali language were displayed in using mediums of copper, silver, and gold records. In Korea, nineteen hinged gold plates told of the Buddhist scriptures. In Italy and France, the museums even displayed ancient commercial records of families, a common procedure until the 16th century. The museums in Jerusalem display many silver scrolls and some inscribed gold plaques used to cover the lips of the deceased. The Louvre Museum in Paris, France, displays large metal columns covered with writing; stone boxes containing copper plates; as well as the oldest example of writing on metal, dated 2450 B.C.

Ancient Writing on Bronze
Courtesy National Archaeological Museum
Athens, Greece

Writing on Ancient Plaque
of Djokha Umma

This small gold plate, 2½ × 1½ inches, is named for Djokha Umma, Iraq, where it was discovered in 1895 by an Arab and acquired the next year by the Louvre. Dating from 2450 B.C. and written in Akkadian, it is one of the oldest examples of writing on metal. This plaque was discovered in the foundation of a sacred building erected by Djokha Umma's queen. The author filmed the plate at the Department of Oriental Antiquities in the Louvre, in Paris. Several other metal plates with writing are on display in the same museum.

Silver Metal Scroll, c. A.D. 400, Bethany, Israel

This beautiful silver scroll, dating from approximately A.D. 400, was discovered in Bethany in 1968, inscribed in Greek and Coptic. Measuring 7¼ × 2⅛ inches, it contains a magical text from a gnostic-like group around Jerusalem. (LDS Information Center, Salt Lake City, Utah)

Shalmanezer III Gold Tablet

A gold tablet found near the source of the Tigris River, referring to Shalanezer III who reigned 859-825 B.C. The tablet describes a series of conquests and the cities where sacrifices were performed. The tablet is at the University of Chicago Oriental Institute. (Ariel L. Crowley, Metal Record Plates in Ancient Times, 1947, pp. 6, 7)

Ancient Writing on Lead Plate
Courtesy National Archaeological Museum
Athens, Greece

An especially lovely example of ancient writing on metal plates is the Korean Keumgangkyeong-pan, nineteen golden plates containing the Diamond Sutra from Buddhist scriptures engraved in Chinese calligraphy. Measuring 14.8×13.7 inches, they were hinged and could be folded on top of each other, then secured by two golden bands wrapped around the plates. During the eighth century, they were placed in a bronze box and buried under a five-story pagoda at Wanggungni, Chollabuk province, South Korea where they were discovered in December 1965. (National Museum, Seoul)

Inscribed gold plaques to cover the lips of the dead

Writing on metal pillar c. 1100 A.D.
Located in the Louvre, Paris, France.

Pali in Burmese Script
India plates covered with gold enameled black writing Kamavaca Text
Courtesy British Museum

In the 3rd and early 2nd millennia B.C., in northern and western India, an urban culture known as the Indus civilization flourished. In many respects it was akin to its contemporaries in Egypt and Mesopotamia. India's literature is thought to begin about 1500 B.C. with a collection of hymns called Rig Veda composed by a people called Aryans. Their language is called Vedic, and is the most ancient form of Sanskrit, the classical language of India.

The Aryans were a branch of the Indo-European tribes who migrated within Europe and the Middle East. Sanskrit is thus related to Greek and Latin. Sanskrit was used exclusively until about A.D. 1300 in India. Pali was regarded as a vulgar tongue developed from Sanskrit. Southern India developed a language called Tamil. (Department of Orient Manuscripts and Printed Books, The British Library, British Museum, London, England.)

Also from India, two Maunggun gold plates were written in the Pali language, and inscribed with three lines of characters on one side only. The weight of the first plate is 110 grains, and the second is 148 grains.

The plates were found in a brick by some workers digging foundations for a new pagoda at Maunggun Village, near Hmawza, in the Prome district. They were sent by Sr. Frederick Fryer, the Lt. Governor of Burma, to Dr. Hultzsch for transmission to the British Museum in London.

The inscriptions contain quotations from the Buddhist scriptures, and date from the first centuries A.D. (Maung Tun Nyein, "Maunggun Gold Plates," Epigraphia Indica, 5 (1898-1899), p. 101.)

A grant written in Sanskrit (in Grantham characters) and Tamil (Vatteruttu characters) referring to the gift of a village called Velvikudi. Found in Tamilnadu, India, A.D. 769. It is noted that the use of rings to bind the plates were used.

Copper Plate Grant in Sanskrit in Devanagri, 12th Century A.D.
Courtesy British Museum

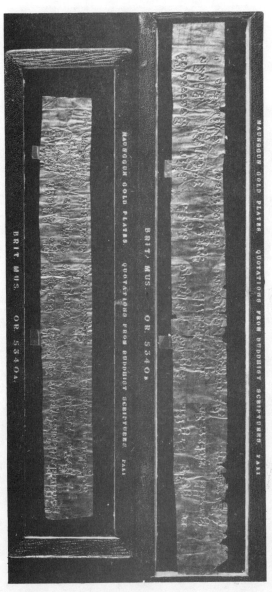

Maunggun Gold Plates
Courtesy British Museum

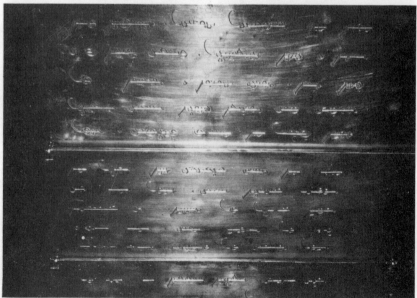

A set of ancient gold plates on display in the Palace Museum in the Forbidden City of Peking, China.

In 1982, two laborers (a man and a woman) engaged in excavations at the Jetavanarama site in the historic city of Anuradhapura, 190 kilometers northeast of Colombo, Sri Lanka, found some metal plates hidden beneath fragments of a broken clay pot. The woman, Padmawathie, and the man, Somapala, made this discovery on December 18, 1982.

The seven gold plates, which they found, measured 63 centimeters long, 5.8 centimeters wide, and 0.576 centimeters thick. Together they weighed more than 2 kilometers. The gold alone is worth $62,000.

Munugoda Hewage Sirisoma, assistant commissioner of archaeology in Sri Lanka, said that the script is 9th century Sinhala, but the language is Sanskrit. Inscribed on the plates are parts of a Mahayana sutra (a philosophical discourse of the Buddha with his disciples) and is called Pragna Paramitha. These seven plates are thought to be a copy of an original version imported from India about 1400 years ago. Sirisonia thinks that there should be more than 100 plates, and is very optimistic about future finds. Photographs are not available at this writing.

Containers for Writing Materials

The Dead Sea Scrolls were found in large pottery jars. The metal plates of Darius were found in stone foundation boxes. Joseph Smith's claim that he found the gold plates in a stone box was a very unique claim in his day. Over fifty stone boxes have been found in the Americas containing valuable articles, as well as written records. Containers for valuables certainly are varied; however, it is interesting that the burial in stone boxes have a coincidence in the parallel of the Old World and the New World.

The stone box pictured here (presently located in the Louvre Museum in Paris) was originally discovered in the foundation of the Temple of Dagan and contained inscribed copper plates. The date of the plates is about 3000 B.C.

Stone Box
Found in foundation of the Temple of Dagan
Contains copper inscribed plates
3000 B.C.

Limestone chest with inscriptions found at Balawat

A limestone box with inscriptions on clay tablets was found at Balawat. This box was found in Sippar containing inscriptions dating back to 626-605 B.C.

Stone box containing inscriptions found at Sippar, 626-605 B.C.

Shown is one of over 50 stone boxes that has been found in the Americas, now located in the Mexico City Museum of Anthropology.

New World
Stone Box

Conclusion

In 1830 Joseph Smith wrote that the ancient inhabitants of the Western Hemisphere were of Hebrew origin; that they had left a number of metallic plates inscribed in an ancient language which he (Joseph Smith) was allowed to translate by the power of God. This claim was considered by his critics to be absolute nonsense, not only because of unbelief concerning the supernatural source of these materials, but also because it didn't happen to fall within the pale of current archaeological opinion. Scientists of the time insisted that the ancient peoples of North and South America were not of Hebrew origin, did not leave a written language, and if they had, would certainly not have left it on metal plates.

Since that time, however, a number of artifacts have been discovered which seem to substantiate Joseph Smith's claim. Yet people have rather steadfastly refused to accept the idea that these artifacts might support the existence of literacy among the pre-Columbian Americans.

After approximately 150 years, public and scholarly opinion are finally beginning to concede the possibility that writing did indeed exist among the ancient Americans. While the author has been waiting for this shift to occur among those groups who place little credence in the Book of Mormon, he has been collecting every available evidence to support his belief in the existence of such writing. His own findings and the findings of others not only establish the fact that writing did exist in ancient America, but they also indicate that metal plates were frequently used as a medium for this writing and that the writings themselves often indicated Old World origins.

Although the existence of writing in the Eastern hemisphere has been traced as far back as 3000 B.C., claims of the existence of writing in ancient America began, so far as we know, with Joseph Smith in 1830. For the most part, archaeologists in America have found it necessary to rely on artifacts (rather than the written word) in order to reconstruct the family life, government, and religious beliefs of the ancestors of the American Indian. The only other sources of information concerning these people have been the writings of the early Spanish chroniclers, as well as the observations of Indians who, upon becoming literate, recorded the oral traditions and legends of their fathers.

Joseph Smith's 1830 declaration, then, was archaeologically significant. Since that time, however, hundreds of examples of writing on metal plates have been discovered worldwide. In addition, writings in various forms — linear symbols, glyphs, alphabet, picture — have been found in all parts of America, on a variety of mediums, ranging from stone tablets to crude forms of paper and metal.

In 1963, a pamphlet was published by The Church of Jesus Christ of Latter-day Saints, written by Franklin S. Harris, entitled "Gold Plates Used Anciently." In it he listed sixty-three individual sets of metal plates located in various museums and gathered from the Old World. A catalogue of writing on metal plates has been made by H. Curtis Wright ("Ancient Burials of Metallic Foundation Documents in Stone Boxes," December 1982).

The Mormon belief of the antiquity of writing:

Adam had a book of remembrance	Moses 6:5
Adam taught his children to write	Moses 6:6
Enoch wrote	Moses 6:45-46
	D&C 107:56-57
Abraham wrote and those before him	Abraham 1:28, 31
Jaredites wrote (2400 B.C.)	Ether 1:1-4
Joseph (who was sold into Egypt)	
wrote	Millennial Star 3:47
Moses wrote	1 Nephi 5:10-13

In the writings of ancient Egypt, Osiris is mentioned in many myths and legends. R. L. Rundle Clark records part of one of the descriptions, as written on a "tablet of Copper," and explains that "Monarchy was founded by the Creator upon the first land to emerge from the Abyss and its rules drawn up on a metal tablet by Ptah-tenen, the High God . . ." (R. T. Rundle Clark, *Myth and Symbol in Ancient Egypt*, p. 175).

Guppy records that "The use of bronze by the Greeks and Romans as a material upon which to engrave votive inscriptions, laws, treaties, and other official documents is established by various authorities . . . Roman military diplomas . . . consisted of two square plates hinged together with rings . . . Plutarch mentions a golden book in the treasury of the Sisyonians at Delphi . . ." (Henry Guppy, *Human Records: A Survey*, Bulletin of John Rylands Library 27, 1942-43, pp. 197, 198).

As the results of this study have indicated, scholars were apparently too hasty in claiming that there was no writing among the ancient inhabitants of the New World. They were equally hasty in scoffing at the idea of possible Hebraic origins and the use of metal as an instrument for the preservation of written language. Consequently, Joseph Smith's account of finding a stone box containing ancient writing on gold plates bound with rings is highly plausible, in the light of modern research on ancient writing in the Old and the New World.

Acknowledgments

Special thanks to the following museums for their cooperation:

Korea National Museum, Seoul, Korea
Archaeological Museum, Teheran, Iran
Rockefeller Archaeological Museum, Jerusalem, Israel
The Hashemite Kingdom of Jordan, Amman, Jordan
The National Archaeological Museum, Athens, Greece
The National Museum of Villa Guilia, Roma, Italy
Museum, Palazzo dei Consoli, Gubbio, Italy
Vatican Museum, Rome, Italy
Museo do America, Madrid, Spain
National Archaeological Museum, Madrid, Spain
Musee de Louvre, Paris, France
Bibliotheque Nationale, Paris, France
Musee de Homme, Paris, France
British Museum, London, England

Photographs of ancient gold plates in Peking courtesy of LaMar C. Berrett. All other photographs are the author's except where acknowledgment is given.

Appendix

Following are descriptions and listings of other ancient metal plates which were found in the Old World:

Gold Plate (Egypt)

This is a small plate, 2" × 6", written in Greek characters on gold. It is in honor of a dedication of a temple to Osiris by Ptolemy Eurgetes and Berenice (242-222 B.C.). It is currently in the British Museum.

Gordon B. Hinckley, "Metal Plates in the British Museum," in the *Improvement Era*, Vol. 39, p. 154 (1936).

Javanese Gold Plates (Indonesia)

Two thin gold plates attached together, containing a letter in Javanese script, dated A.D. 1768. Now in the British Museum.

F. S. Harris, *The Book of Mormon Message and Evidences* (Salt Lake City, 1953), chapter 10.

Himyaritic Brass Tablets (Yemen)

Sir Richard F. Burton, the renowned traveler, said that "of late years Himyaritic inscriptions upon brass tablets have been forwarded from Yemen in Arabia to the British Museum." Presumably, they are still in the British Museum.

Sir Richard F. Burton, *City of the Saints*, 1861, p. 488.

Silver Koran Plates (Turkey)

This is a group of several plates, about 4½" × 3" long, containing a portion of the Koran in elegant Arabic script. The plates form a book over an inch thick when stacked one on top of another. They are in the Evkaf Museum in Istanbul.

F. S. Harris, *The Book of Mormon Message and Evidences*, p. 99.

Hmawza Book (Burma)

A gold-leaf book of twenty numbered pages found at Hmawza (Old Prome) in 1926. The book dates from the fifth century A.D. It was patterned after the palm leaf manuscripts common in India at the time. Each leaf has two perforations through which they are connected by heavy gold wire. The book contains assorted Buddhist writings, kind of an anthology.

Hihar Ranjan Ray, *Journal of the Greater Indian Society*, 7 (1939), p. 47.

"The gold-leaf Pali manuscript of Old Prome" in *Report of the Superintendent, Archaeological Survey of Burma*, 1938-1939, p. 12.

Mattapad Plates of Damodaravarman (India)

Peddavegi Plates of Salankavana Naudivarman (India)

Kautern Plates of Vyayaskandavarman (India)

Chikulla Plates of Vikramendravarma (India)

Koroshanda Copper Plates of Viskharvarma (India)

Komarti Plates of Chandavarma (India)

G. Ramadas, *Journal of Bihar Research Society*, XXXIV (1948), pp. 34, 35.

Kesarbeda Copper Plates (India)

Three copper plates strung together on a copper ring. The plates, written on both sides, are inscribed, perforated, and linked by the ring. They date to A.D. 324. They are a royal charter concerning the government of the land.

G. Ramadas, *Journal of Bihar Research Society*, XXXIV (1948), p. 23.

Karen Inscription Plate (Thailand)

A plate formed of two separate plates, one of copper and the other apparently of gold, welded together back to back. The language is not known, but the plates in the 19th century were

the "talisman by which the chief held his power over the people."
It is logical that the plates were originally a royal charter.

A. Bunker, "On a Karen Inscription Plate," *Journal of the American
Oriental Society*, X (1872), pp. 172-177.

Boss of Tarkondemos (Syria)

The "boss" consisted of a round silver plate which probably
once covered the knob of a staff or a dagger. In 1872 it was in
the collection of Alexander Jovanoff, a numismatist in Con-
stantinople. Its present location is not given. The "boss" bears
a peculiar Hittite figure flanked on both sides by writing in
Hittite characters. It also carries an inscription in ancient Assyrian
cuneiform. First described by A. D. Mordtmann in the *Journal of
the German Oriental Society* in 1872.

G. A. Barton, *Archaeology of the Bible*, 6th edition, 1933, figure 26
and page 87.

Aljustrel Bronze Tablets (Portugal)

These are Roman mining documents. There are two tablets. The
first was found in 1876 and the second in 1907. Each of the
tablets consists of the two plates together, so there are four
plates in all. They contain rules and laws governing the mines,
the use of public baths, cutting of hair, fulling of cloth, and
special privileges due school teachers.

A. D. Cummings, W. R. Chalmers, and H. B. Mattingly, "A Roman
mining document," *Mine and Quarry Engineering*, August 1956, p. 339.

Copper or Bronze Plate in Hebrew (Lebanon-Phoenicia)

Dates from the 12th century B.C. It was a letter entirely secular
in nature.

J. Obermann, "An Early Phoenician Political Document," *Journal of
Biblical Literature*, 58 (1939), pp. 229-231.

Wm. F. Albright, *Bulletin of the American Schools of Oriental Research*, 73, p. 9 ff.

Byblos Bronze Plates (Lebanon)

A collection of bronze plates with texts in a curious variant of Egyptian. Nibley calls it mysterious "reformed Egyptian." Byblos is the current city of Jubayl, Lebanon. The bronze tablets were found by Dunand, and date from the 18th century B.C. Albright calls their inscription "pseudo-hieroglyphic."

Hugh W. Nibley, *Lehi in the Desert*, p. 120.

Artaxerxes II, Hamadan Gold Tablet (Iran)

A gold tablet found at Hamadan, Iran. It contains 20 lines in Old Persian. The text begins with a praise to Ahuramazda, the supreme god. A brief genealogy follows: The author, Artaxerxes the king, declares himself the son of Hystaspes and a citizen of Achaemenia. He then says that the kingship was bestowed on him from god, and the tablet closes with a prayer that Ahuramazda will protect him and his house. At one time this plate was in the Musee Cernuschi, Paris. Its whereabouts at present is not known. As of 1948 it was owned by a Mr. Vidal of New York.

Arsames Gold Tablet (Iran)

A gold tablet in three pieces written in Old Persian found at Hamadan, Iran. This text begins with a brief genealogy of the king, Arsames. He states that he rules by divine right, and he concludes with a prayer that the supreme god Ahuramazda will protect his house, his horses, and his lands. At one time this palate was in the Musee Cernushci in Paris, but its present location is uncertain. In 1948 it was in the collection of a Mr. Vidal in New York City.

Sicilian Gold Plate (Italy)

Discovered in 1876 on Sicily. The writing was unidentified for almost a century. In 1964 it was identified as Hebrew.

U. Schmoll in Zeitschrift der dt. Morgenland, Gesellschaft, 113 (1964), pp. 512-514.

Venice and Bologna Lead Plates (Italy)

Lead tablets used to inscribe historical and diplomatic records in the 14th and 15th centuries. Some examples from Venice and Bologna may even have been used after the invention of the printing press.

Henry Guppy, "Human Records, a survey of their history from the beginning," in *Bulletin of the John Rylands Library*, 27 (1942-1943), p. 197.

Bibliography

American Heritage of America. New York: American Heritage Publishing Co., Inc., 1961.

Bacon, Edward, ed. *Vanished Civilizations of the Ancient World.* New York: McGraw-Hill Book Co., Inc., 1963.

Brockbank, Thomas W. *Improvement Era.* Salt Lake City: The Church of Jesus Christ of Latter-day Saints, 1914.

Brown, D. S. *The Catawba Indians.* University of South Carolina, 1966.

Brown, J. M. *The Riddle of the Pacific.* London: T. F. Unwin, Ltd., 1925.

Clark, R. T. Rundle. *Myth and Symbol in Ancient Egypt.* New York: Grove Press, Inc., 1960.

Davidson, A. B. *Hebrew Syntax,* 3rd ed. Edinburgh: T & T Clark, 1950.

De Roo, Peter. *America Before Columbus.* New York: J. P. Lippincott Co., 1900.

Gamboa, Pedro Sarmiento de. *History of the Incas* (1575, in works issued by the Hakluyt Society, Series No. XXII, Cambridge, 1907). As cited in Milton R. Hunter, *Christ in Ancient America.* Salt Lake City: Deseret Book Co., 1959.

Gaur, Albertine. *Writing Materials of the East.* London: The British Library, British Museum.

Gelb, I. J. *A Study of Writing.* Chicago: The University of Chicago Press, 1969.

Gomora, Lopez de. *Historia General de las Indias, Historiators Primitivos de Indias.*

Gordon, Cyrus H. *Before Columbus.* New York: Crown Publishers, 1971.

Guppy, Henry. *Human Records: A Survey.* Bulletin of John Rylands Library 27, 1942-1943.

Haines, Elijah M. *The American Indian.* Chicago: The Massinnagan Co., 1888.

Harrison, Park J. *Nature,* vol. 10. London & New York: MacMillan and Co., 1874.

Heyerdahl, Thor. *American Indians in the Pacific.* London: George Allen and Unwin, Ltd., Ruskin House, 1952.

Honore, Pierre. *In Quest of the White God.* London: Hutchinson & Co., 1961.

Houck, Louis. *A History of Missouri.* Chicago: R. R. Donnelley and Sons Co., 1908.

Irwin, Constance. *Fair Gods and Stone Faces.* New York: St. Martin's Press, 1963.

Jakeman, Wells. *The Ancient Civilizations of Middle America.*

Jara, Victor de la. *Introduction el Estudio de la Escritera de los Inkas.* Lima, Peru: INIDE, 1975.

Josephy, Alvin M., Jr. *The Indian Heritage of America.* New York: Alfred A. Knopf, Inc., 1968.

Killer, Rev. P. Conrad. *The German Colonies in South Russia.* Canada: Western Producer, 1968.

Lothrop, S. K. *Treasures of Ancient America.* Cleveland: World Publishing Co., 1964.

Mason, J. Alden. *The Ancient Civilizations of Peru.* Baltimore: Penguin Books, 1957.

McFadyen, John. *Key to Introductory Hebrew Grammar,* 3rd ed., Edinburgh: T & T Clark, 1951.

Montestnos, Fernando. Edited by Philip Answorth Means. *Memorias Antiquas Historiales del Peru.* London: Bedford Press, 1920.

Peet, Stephen. *Prehistoric America.* Chicago: Office of the American Antiquarian, 1892.

Plutarchus. Quaestiones convivales 5.2.

Pottier, Bernard. *The Indian Languages of America* in Research. New York, 1977.

Priest, Josiah. *American Antiquities,* 3rd ed. revised. New York: Hoffman and White, 1833.

Proceedings of the Tenth Pacific Science Congress. Honolulu, 1961.

Quast—Conviv. v., pp. 2-10.

Reynolds, George. *A Complete Concordance of the Book of Mormon.* Salt Lake City: Deseret Book Co., 1957.

Rivero, Mariano Eduardo de and Dr. Juan Diego de Tschudi. *Antiguedodes Pervanos.* Vienna: Imprenta de la Corte y del Estado, 1851.

Saville, Marshall Howard. *The Goldsmith's Art in Ancient Mexico.* New York: Museum of the American Indian, Heyefoundation, 1920.

Skinner, J. Ralston. *Key to the Hebrews: Egyptian Mystery in the Sources of Measure.* 1875.

Taylor, Albert P. *Under Hawaiian Skies.* Honolulu: Advertiser Publishing Co., Ltd., 1926.

Thompson, J. Eric. *Handbook of Middle American Indian,* vol. 3. Austin: University of Texas Press, 1964-1966.

Torquemada, Juan de. *Monarquia Indiana.* 1615.

Tozer, A. M., ed. *Relacion de las Cosa de Yucatan.* Cambridge: Peabody Museum, 1940.

Ventura, Gilda Corgorno. *Revisita de la Biblio teca Naxcional Instituto de Culture.* Peru, 1977.

Verrill, Hyatt. *America's Ancient Civilizations.* New York: B. P. Putnam's Sons, 1953.

Von Hagen, Victor Wolfgang. *The Ancient Sun Kingdoms of the Americas.* New York: The World Publishing Co., 1961.

Wissler, Clark. *Indians of the United States.* New York: Doubleday & Company, 1966.

Wright, H. Curtis. "Ancient Burials of Metallic Foundation Documents in Stone Boxes." University of Illinois Graduate School of Library and International Science, Number 157, 1982.

Ximenez, Francisco Fray. *Historia de la Provincia de San Vicente de Chiapa y Guatemala.* Guatemala, 1929.

Periodicals

Scientific American. May 1978.
Science 2. May 1971.
Western Reserve Historical Society Tracts. February 9, 1872.
SEHA Newsletter, 112.0.

Theses

Bramwell, E. Craig. "Hebrew Idioms in the Small Plates of Nephi." Unpublished Master's thesis. Brigham Young University, 1960.